Jesus

Also 'In My Own Words':

Cardinal Basil Hume

Leo Tolstoy

Mother Teresa

Pope John XXIII

Pope John Paul II

Jesus

In My Own Words

Compiled and edited by
TERESA DE BERTODANO

Hodder & Stoughton
LONDON   SYDNEY   AUCKLAND

First published in Great Britain in 2000

The right of Teresa de Bertodano to be identified as the Editor of the Work
has been asserted by her in accordance with the
Copyright, Designs and Patents Act 1988.

10 9 8 7 6 5 4 3 2 1

British Library Cataloguing in Publication Data
A record for this book is available from the British Library

ISBN 0 340 756837

Typeset in Adobe Goudy Old Style by
Strathmore Publishing Services, London N7

Printed and bound in Great Britain by
Clays Ltd, St Ives plc

Hodder and Stoughton
A Division of Hodder Headline Ltd
338 Euston Road
London NW1 3BH

CONTENTS

INTRODUCTION

The most beloved of all Christian prayers is undoubtedly the Lord's Prayer or 'Our Father', given to us by Jesus Christ himself. Jesus's own life of prayer and his preaching were in perfect harmony, and the totality of his teaching is contained within the nine phrases of the Lord's Prayer. It is not therefore surprising that we can arrange so many of his words under those nine headings – as has been done in *Jesus: In My Own Words*.

The first Christians left us the words of Jesus in two forms. The Gospels that bear the names of Matthew, Mark and Luke report the words of Jesus from his earthly ministry which ended with his death and resurrection – probably no later than AD 30. These three Gospels are generally thought to have been completed between AD 65 and AD 80. The Gospel of John probably appeared in its final form towards the end of the first century. It conveys a deeper perception of the words of Jesus as heard, prayed over and developed in the heart of the gospel-writer during the half-century following the resurrection. *Jesus: In My Own Words* distinguishes between the reportage of the Gospels of Matthew, Mark and Luke on the one hand and, on the other, the recollections of the writer of John's Gospel, preserved and elaborated over nearly seventy years. The author of John's Gospel hears the words of Jesus resonating in his heart. We, today, need to hear both the words of the earthly Jesus speaking to us through the Gospels of Matthew, Mark and Luke and the words of the risen and ever-present Jesus delivered to us in the Gospel of John.

From the Gospel of Luke we learn the first recorded words of Jesus at the age of twelve when he came from Nazareth to Jerusalem to visit the Temple. But almost all the public words of Jesus arise from the ministry which opened with his baptism in the River Jordan by John the Baptist. There followed a period of prayer and fasting in the desert during which Jesus was tempt-ed by Satan. He left the desert to begin a wandering ministry for a period of between eighteen months and four years which took him to villages in Galilee, to non-Jewish Samaria as well as to other places outside Jewish territory – and finally to Jerusalem.

Jesus began his ministry by announcing that he was

bringing to his hearers the Good News of the kingdom of God. Between the opening of his ministry and the final week of his life, he told stories or parables about the kingdom of God and encapsulated the kingdom message in the Beatitudes, such as 'Blessed are the poor in spirit'. Jesus taught us how to relate to God and to one another and announced the final coming of the divine kingdom. At the end of his life he celebrated a final meal with his chosen group of followers and prayed in the Garden of Gethsemane where he was arrested. The religious authorities brought him to trial before the Roman Governor, Pontius Pilate, and he was executed between two criminals.

To a large extent, the order in which Jesus taught his parables and delivered his teaching is lost to us. We simply do not know, for example, whether the tale of the Prodigal Son came before or after the parable of the Good Samaritan. The four gospel-writers arranged the text in an order that each found to be most appropriate. No matter what the actual order of delivery, the words of Jesus continue to challenge our ways of thinking and of living. Back in the first century they challenged Peter, Mary Magdalene and other followers of Jesus to the extent that they made radical changes in their lifestyles and dedicated their remaining years to following him. The words and deeds of Jesus proved so offensive to some powerful religious leaders that they persuaded Pontius Pilate to use his authority to sentence him to death as a threat to Roman authority and a criminally false religious leader. The words of Jesus continue to resonate down the centuries, inspiring some people to give up everything to follow him while others find his teaching deeply threatening and offensive.

As we enter the third millennium, we are blessed with a rich variety of English translations of the Bible. Some are particularly suited to public reading and divine worship while others are more appropriate for private study and others, again, for the instruction of children. The 1978 New International Version of the Bible, as well as giving us a very accurate translation from the original languages – Hebrew, Greek and Aramaic – follows the Authorised or King James Version of 1611 in a tradition with which many readers are familiar.

For me, personally, it has been a grace and a privilege to prepare this book and thus to revisit the words of Jesus in the four Gospels. I hope and pray that readers of *Jesus: In My Own Words* will be nourished as I have been.

TERESA DE BERTODANO

OUR FATHER

Father,
hallowed be your name,
your kingdom come.
Give us each day our daily bread.
Forgive us our sins,
for we also forgive everyone who sins against us.
And lead us not into temptation.

LUKE 11:2-4

*After the Feast [of the Passover] was over, while his
parents were returning home, the boy Jesus stayed behind
in Jerusalem, but they were unaware of it ...*

*W*hy were you searching for me? ... Didn't you
know I had to be in my Father's house?

LUKE 2:49

I tell you that if two of you on earth agree about anything you ask for, it will be done for you by my Father
in heaven. For where two or three come together in
my name, there am I with them.

MATTHEW 18:19-20

3

Simon Peter [said], 'You are the Christ, the Son of the living God.'

... *B*lessed are you, Simon son of Jonah, for this was not revealed to you by man, but by my Father in heaven.

MATTHEW 16:17

*W*hoever acknowledges me before men, I will also acknowledge him before my Father in heaven. But whoever disowns me before men, I will disown him before my Father in heaven.

MATTHEW 10:32-3

You are not to be called 'Rabbi', for you have only one Master and you are all brothers. And do not call anyone on earth 'father', for you have one Father, and he is in heaven. Nor are you to be called 'teacher', for you have one Teacher, the Christ. The greatest among you will be your servant. For whoever exalts himself will be humbled, and whoever humbles himself will be exalted.

MATTHEW 23:8-12

Look at the birds of the air; they do not sow or reap or store away in barns, and yet your heavenly Father feeds them. Are you not much more valuable than they?

MATTHEW 6:26

*A*re not two sparrows sold for a penny? Yet not one of them will fall to the ground apart from the will of your Father. And even the very hairs of your head are numbered. So don't be afraid; you are worth more than many sparrows.

MATTHEW 10:29-31

*W*hen you give to the needy, do not let your left hand know what your right hand is doing, so that your giving may be in secret. Then your Father, who sees what is done in secret, will reward you.

MATTHEW 6:3-4

*T*here was a man who had two sons. The younger one said to his father, 'Father, give me my share of the estate.' So he divided his property between them.

Not long after that, the younger son got together all he had, set off for a distant country and there squandered his wealth in wild living. After he had spent everything, there was a severe famine in that whole country, and he began to be in need. So he went and hired himself out to a citizen of that country, who sent him to his fields to feed pigs. He longed to fill his stomach with the pods that the pigs were eating, but no-one gave him anything

When he came to his senses, he said, 'How many of my father's hired men have food to spare, and here I am starving to death! I will set out and go back to my father and say to him: Father, I have sinned against heaven and against you. I am no longer worthy to be called your son; make me like one of your hired men.' So he got up and went to his father …

LUKE 15:11-20

7

... *W*hile [the younger son] was still a long way off, his father saw him and was filled with compassion for him; he ran to his son, threw his arms around him and kissed him.

The son said to him, 'Father, I have sinned against heaven and against you. I am no longer worthy to be called your son.'

But the father said to his servants, 'Quick! Bring the best robe and put it on him. Put a ring on his finger and sandals on his feet. Bring the fattened calf and kill it. Let's have a feast and celebrate. For this son of mine was dead and is alive again; he was lost and is found.' So they began to celebrate.

Meanwhile, the older son was in the field. When he came near the house, he heard music and dancing. So he called one of the servants and asked him what was going on. 'Your brother has come,' he replied, 'and your father has killed the fattened calf because he has him back safe and sound' ...

LUKE 15:20-7

... *T*he older brother became angry and refused to go in. So his father went out and pleaded with him. But he answered his father, 'Look! All these years I've been slaving for you and never disobeyed your orders. Yet you never gave me even a young goat so I could celebrate with my friends. But when this son of yours who has squandered your property with prostitutes comes home, you kill the fattened calf for him!'

'My son,' the father said, 'you are always with me, and everything I have is yours. But we had to celebrate and be glad, because this brother of yours was dead and is alive again; he was lost and is found.'

LUKE 15:28-33

*W*hat do you think? If a man owns a hundred sheep, and one of them wanders away, will he not leave the ninety-nine on the hills and go to look for the one that wandered off? And if he finds it, I tell you the truth, he is happier about that one sheep than about the ninety-nine that did not wander off. In the same way your Father in heaven is not willing that any of these little ones should be lost.

MATTHEW 18:12-14

9

*S*uppose a woman has ten silver coins and loses one. Does she not light a lamp, sweep the house and search carefully until she finds it? And when she finds it, she calls her friends and neighbours together and says, 'Rejoice with me; I have found my lost coin.' In the same way, I tell you, there is rejoicing in the presence of the angels of God over one sinner who repents.

LUKE 15:8-10

*S*ee that you do not look down on one of these little ones. For I tell you that their angels in heaven always see the face of my Father in heaven.

MATTHEW 18:10

*A*ll things have been committed to me by my Father. No-one knows the Son except the Father, and no-one knows the Father except the Son and those to whom the Son chooses to reveal him.

MATTHEW 11:27

*W*hen you pray, go into your room, close the door and pray to your Father, who is unseen. Then your Father, who sees what is done in secret, will reward you. And when you pray, do not keep on babbling like pagans, for they think they will be heard because of their many words. Do not be like them, for your Father knows what you need before you ask him.

MATTHEW 6:6-8

*A*sk and it will be given to you; seek and you will find; knock and the door will be opened to you. For everyone who asks receives; he who seeks finds; and to him who knocks, the door will be opened.

LUKE 11:9-10

When they came to the place called the Skull, there they crucified him ...

𝓕ather, forgive them, for they do not know what they are doing.

LUKE 23:34

𝓕ather, into your hands I commit my spirit.

LUKE 23:46

A time is coming and has now come when the true worshippers will worship the Father in spirit and truth, for they are the kind of worshippers the Father seeks. God is spirit, and his worshippers must worship in spirit and in truth.

JOHN 4:23-4

*T*he Son can do nothing by himself; he can do only what he sees his Father doing, because whatever the Father does the Son also does. For the Father loves the Son and shows him all he does.

JOHN 5:19-20

*J*ust as the Father raises the dead and gives them life, even so the Son gives life to whom he is pleased to give it. Moreover, the Father judges no-one, but has entrusted all judgment to the Son, that all may honour the Son just as they honour the Father. He who does not honour the Son does not honour the Father who sent him.

JOHN 5:21-3

*A*s the Father has life in himself, so he has granted the Son to have life in himself. And he has given him authority to judge because he is the Son of Man.

JOHN 5:26-7

*M*y Father's will is that everyone who looks to the Son and believes in him shall have eternal life, and I will raise him up at the last day.

JOHN 6:40

*N*o-one can come to me unless the Father who sent me draws him, and I will raise him up at the last day. It is written in the Prophets: 'They will all be taught by God.' Everyone who listens to the Father and learns from him comes to me. No-one has seen the Father except the one who is from God; only he has seen the Father. I tell you the truth, he who believes has everlasting life.

JOHN 6:44-7

*W*hen you have lifted up the Son of Man, then you will know that I am [the one I claim to be] and that I do nothing on my own but speak just what the Father has taught me. The one who sent me is with me; he has not left me alone, for I always do what pleases him.

JOHN 8:28-9

I am the gate for the sheep. All who ever came before me were thieves and robbers, but the sheep did not listen to them. I am the gate; whoever enters through me will be saved. He will come in and go out, and find pasture. The thief comes only to steal and kill and destroy; I have come that they may have life, and have it to the full.

I am the good shepherd. The good shepherd lays down his life for the sheep.

The hired hand is not the shepherd who owns the sheep. So when he sees the wolf coming, he abandons the sheep and runs away. Then the wolf attacks the flock and scatters it. The man runs away because he is a hired hand and cares nothing for the sheep …

JOHN 10:7-13

... *I* am the good shepherd; I know my sheep and my sheep know me – just as the Father knows me and I know the Father – and I lay down my life for the sheep. I have other sheep that are not of this sheep pen. I must bring them also. They too will listen to my voice and there shall be one flock and one shepherd. The reason my Father loves me is that I lay down my life – only to take it up again. No-one takes it from me, but I lay it down of my own accord. I have authority to lay it down and authority to take it up again. This command I received from my Father.

JOHN 10:14-18

*T*he miracles I do in my Father's name speak for me, but you do not believe because you are not my sheep. My sheep listen to my voice; I know them, and they follow me. I give them eternal life, and they shall never perish; no-one can snatch them out of my hand. My Father, who has given them to me, is greater than all; no-one can snatch them out of my Father's hand. I and the Father are one.

JOHN 10:25-30

*E*ven though you do not believe me, believe the miracles, that you may know and understand that the Father is in me, and I in the Father.

JOHN 10:38

I am the way and the truth and the life. No-one comes to the Father except through me. If you really knew me, you would know my Father as well. From now on, you do know him and have seen him.

JOHN 14:6-7

*A*nyone who has seen me has seen the Father.

JOHN 14:9

*H*ow can you say, 'Show us the Father'? Don't you believe that I am in the Father, and that the Father is in me? The words I say to you are not just my own. Rather, it is the Father, living in me, who is doing his work. Believe me when I say that I am in the Father and the Father is in me; or at least believe on the evidence of the miracles themselves. I tell you the truth, anyone who has faith in me will do what I have been doing. He will do even greater things than these, because I am going to the Father. And I will do whatever you ask in my name, so that the Son may bring glory to the Father. You may ask me for anything in my name, and I will do it.

JOHN 14:9-14

*I*f anyone loves me, he will obey my teaching. My Father will love him, and we will come to him and make our home with him. He who does not love me will not obey my teaching. These words you hear are not my own; they belong to the Father who sent me. All this I have spoken while still with you. But the Counsellor, the Holy Spirit, whom the Father will send in my name, will teach you all things and will remind you of everything I have said to you. Peace I leave with you; my peace I give you. I do not give to you as the world gives. Do not let your hearts be troubled and do not be afraid.

JOHN 14:23-7

*Y*ou heard me say, 'I am going away and I am coming back to you.' If you loved me, you would be glad that I am going to the Father, for the Father is greater than I. I have told you now before it happens, so that when it does happen you will believe. I will not speak with you much longer, for the prince of this world is coming. He has no hold on me; but the world must learn that I love the Father and that I do exactly what my Father has commanded me.

JOHN 14:28-31

I am the true vine, and my Father is the gardener. He cuts off every branch in me that bears no fruit, while every branch that does bear fruit he prunes so that it will be even more fruitful. You are already clean because of the word I have spoken to you. Remain in me, and I will remain in you. No branch can bear fruit by itself; it must remain in the vine. Neither can you bear fruit unless you remain in me.

JOHN 15:1-4

*A*s the Father has loved me, so have I loved you. Now remain in my love. If you obey my commands, you will remain in my love, just as I have obeyed my Father's commands and remain in his love. I have told you this so that my joy may be in you and that your joy may be complete. My command is this: Love each other as I have loved you. Greater love has no-one than this, that he lay down his life for his friends. You are my friends if you do what I command. I no longer call you servants, because a servant does not know his master's business. Instead, I have called you friends, for everything that I learned from my Father I have made known to you. You did not choose me, but I chose you and appointed you to go and bear fruit – fruit that will last. Then the Father will give you whatever you ask in my name. This is my command: Love each other.

JOHN 15:9-17

I have been speaking figuratively, a time is coming when I will no longer use this kind of language but will tell you plainly about my Father. In that day you will ask in my name. I am not saying that I will ask the Father on your behalf. No, the Father himself loves you because you have loved me and have believed that I came from God. I came from the Father and entered the world; now I am leaving the world and going back to the Father.

JOHN 16:25-8

Mary Magdalene went to the tomb ... Jesus said to her,

*M*ary, do not hold on to me, for I have not yet returned to the Father. Go instead to my brothers and tell them, 'I am returning to my Father and your Father, to my God and your God.'

JOHN 20:16-17

Hallowed Be

Thy Name

I praise you, Father, Lord of heaven and earth, because you have hidden these things from the wise and learned, and revealed them to little children. Yes, Father, for this was your good pleasure.

LUKE 10:21

The devil took him to a very high mountain and showed him all the kingdoms of the world and their splendour. 'All this I will give you,' he said, 'if you will bow down and worship me.'

*A*way from me, Satan! For it is written: 'Worship the Lord your God, and serve him only.'

MATTHEW 4:10

*Y*ou are the salt of the earth. But if the salt loses its saltiness, how can it be made salty again? It is no longer good for anything, except to be thrown out and trampled by men.

You are the light of the world. A city on a hill cannot be hidden. Neither do people light a lamp and put it under a bowl. Instead they put it on its stand, and it gives light to everyone in the house. In the same way, let your light shine before men, that they may see your good deeds and praise your Father in heaven.

MATTHEW 5:13-16

Jesus saw the rich putting their gifts into the temple treasury. He also saw a poor widow put in two very small copper coins.

*T*his poor widow has put in more than all the others. All these people gave their gifts out of their wealth; but she out of her poverty put in all she had to live on.

LUKE 21:3-4

*N*o-one can serve two masters. Either he will hate the one and love the other, or he will be devoted to the one and despise the other. You cannot serve both God and Money.

MATTHEW 6:24

*T*his is what the kingdom of God is like. A man scatters seed on the ground. Night and day, whether he sleeps or gets up, the seed sprouts and grows, though he does not know how. All by itself the soil produces corn – first the stalk, then the ear, then the full grain in the ear. As soon as the grain is ripe, he puts the sickle to it, because the harvest has come.

MATTHEW 4:26-9

*A*ll things have been committed to me by my Father. No-one knows who the Son is except the Father, and no-one knows who the Father is except the Son and those to whom the Son chooses to reveal him … Blessed are the eyes that see what you see. For I tell you that many prophets and kings wanted to see what you see but did not see it, and to hear what you hear but did not hear it.

LUKE 10:22-6

In the temple courts [Jesus] found men selling ... he made a whip out of cords, and drove all from the temple area ...

*H*ow dare you turn my Father's house into a market!

JOHN 2:16

His disciples asked him, 'Rabbi, who sinned, this man or his parents that he was born blind?'

*N*either this man nor his parents sinned ... but this happened so that the work of God might be displayed in his life.

JOHN 9:3

*T*he hour has come for the Son of Man to be glorified. I tell you the truth, unless a grain of wheat falls to the ground and dies, it remains only a single seed. But if it dies, it produces many seeds. The man who loves his life will lose it, while the man who hates his life in this world will keep it for eternal life. Whoever serves me must follow me; and where I am, my servant also will be. My Father will honour the one who serves me.

Now my heart is troubled, and what shall I say? 'Father, save me from this hour'? No, it was for this very reason I came to this hour. Father, glorify your name!

JOHN 12:23-8

*W*hen a man believes in me, he does not believe in me only, but in the one who sent me. When he looks at me, he sees the one who sent me. I have come into the world as a light, so that no-one who believes in me should stay in darkness.

JOHN 12:44-6

$\mathcal{N}$ow is the Son of Man glorified and God is glorified in him. If God is glorified in him, God will glorify the Son in himself, and will glorify him at once.

JOHN 13:31-2

$\mathcal{I}$ am the vine; you are the branches. If a man remains in me and I in him, he will bear much fruit; apart from me you can do nothing. If anyone does not remain in me, he is like a branch that is thrown away and withers; such branches are picked up, thrown into the fire and burned. If you remain in me and my words remain in you, ask whatever you wish, and it will be given you. This it to my Father's glory, that you bear much fruit, showing yourselves to be my disciples.

JOHN 15:5-8

I have revealed you to those whom you gave me out of the world. They were yours; you gave them to me and they have obeyed your word. Now they know that everything you have given me comes from you. For I gave them the words you gave me and they accepted them. They knew with certainty that I came from you, and they believed that you sent me. I pray for them. I am not praying for the world, but for those you have given me, for they are yours. All I have is yours, and all you have is mine. And glory has come to me through them. I will remain in the world no longer, but they are still in the world, and I am coming to you. Holy Father, protect them by the power of your name – the name you gave me – so that they may be one as we are one. While I was with them, I protected them and kept them safe by that name you gave me. None has been lost except the one doomed to destruction so that Scripture would be fulfilled

JOHN 17:6-12

THY KINGDOM COME

Blessed are you who are poor,
for yours is the kingdom of God.
Blessed are you who hunger now,
for you will be satisfied.
Blessed are you who weep now,
for you will laugh.
Blessed are you when men hate you,
when they exclude you and insult you and reject
your name as evil, because of the Son of Man.

LUKE 6:20-2

*T*he time has come … The kingdom of God is near. Repent and believe the good news!

MARK 1:15

*T*he harvest is plentiful, but the workers are few. Ask the Lord of the harvest, therefore, to send out workers into his harvest field.

LUKE 10:2

*W*hen you see a cloud rising in the west, immediately you say, 'It's going to rain,' and it does. And when the south wind blows, you say, 'It's going to be hot,' and it is. Hypocrites! You know how to interpret the appearance of the earth and the sky. How is it that you don't know how to interpret this present time?

LUKE 12:54-6

Jesus began to speak to the crowd about John [the Baptist].

What did you go out into the desert to see? A reed swayed by the wind? If not, what did you go out to see? A man dressed in fine clothes? No, those who wear expensive clothes and indulge in luxury are in palaces. But what did you go out to see? A prophet? Yes, I tell you, and more than a prophet. This is the one about whom it is written: 'I will send my messenger ahead of you, who will prepare your way before you.' I tell you, among those born of women there is no-one greater than John; yet the one who is least in the kingdom of God is greater than he.

LUKE 7:24-8

*The Pharisees and the teachers of the law … said 'John's
disciples often fast and pray, and so do the disciples of the
Pharisees, but yours go on eating and drinking.'*

Can you make the guests of the bridegroom fast while
he is with them? But the time will come when the
bridegroom will be taken from them; in those days
they will fast.

LUKE 5:34-5

A farmer went out to sow his seed. As he was scatter-
ing the seed, some fell along the path, and the birds
came and ate it up. Some fell on rocky places, where it
did not have much soil. It sprang up quickly, because
the soil was shallow. But when the sun came up, the
plants were scorched, and they withered because they
had no root. Other seed fell among thorns, which grew
up and choked the plants. Still other seed fell on good
soil, where it produced a crop – a hundred, sixty or
thirty times what was sown. He who has ears, let him
hear …

MATTHEW 13:3-9

... *L*isten then to what the parable of the sower means: When anyone hears the message about the kingdom and does not understand it, the evil one comes and snatches away what was sown in his heart. This is the seed sown along the path. The one who received the seed that fell on rocky places is the man who hears the word and at once receives it with joy. But since he has no root, he lasts only a short time. When trouble or persecution comes because of the word, he quickly falls away. The one who received the seed that fell among the thorns is the man who hears the word, but the worries of this life and the deceitfulness of wealth choke it, making it unfruitful. But the one who received the seed that fell on good soil is the man who hears the word and understands it. He produces a crop, yielding a hundred, sixty or thirty times what was sown.

MATTHEW 13:18-23

$\mathcal{T}$he kingdom of heaven is like a man who sowed good seed in his field. But while everyone was sleeping, his enemy came and sowed weeds among the wheat, and went away. When the wheat sprouted and formed ears, then the weeds also appeared.

The owner's servants came to him and said, 'Sir, didn't you sow good seed in your field? Where then did the weeds come from?'

'An enemy did this,' he replied.

The servants asked him, 'Do you want us to go and pull them up?'

'No,' he answered, 'because while you are pulling the weeds, you may root up the wheat with them. Let both grow together until the harvest. At that time I will tell the harvesters: First collect the weeds and tie them in bundles to be burned; then gather the wheat and bring it into my barn' ...

MATTHEW 13:24-30

... *T*he one who sowed the good seed is the Son of Man. The field is the world, and the good seed stands for the sons of the kingdom. The weeds are the sons of the evil one, and the enemy who sows them is the devil. The harvest is the end of the age, and the harvesters are angels.

As the weeds are pulled up and burned in the fire, so it will be at the end of the age. The Son of Man will send out his angels, and they will weed out of his kingdom everything that causes sin and all who do evil. They will throw them into the fiery furnace, where there will be weeping and gnashing of teeth. Then the righteous will shine like the sun in the kingdom of their Father. He who has ears, let him hear.

MATTHEW 13:37-43

*T*he kingdom of heaven is like a net that was let down into the lake and caught all kinds of fish. When it was full, the fishermen pulled it up on the shore. Then they sat down and collected the good fish in baskets, but threw the bad away.

MATTHEW 13:47-8

The kingdom of heaven is like treasure hidden in a field. When a man found it, he hid it again, and then in his joy went and sold all he had and bought that field.

MATTHEW 13:44

The kingdom of heaven is like a merchant looking for fine pearls. When he found one of great value, he went away and sold everything he had and bought it.

MATTHEW 13:45-6

Every teacher of the law who has been instructed about the kingdom of heaven is like the owner of a house who brings out of his storeroom new treasures as well as old.

MATTHEW 13:52

*D*o not worry, saying, 'What shall we eat?' or 'What shall we drink?' or 'What shall we wear?' For the pagans run after all these things, and your heavenly Father knows that you need them. But seek first his kingdom and his righteousness, and all these things will be given to you as well.

MATTHEW 6:31-3

*D*o not store up for yourselves treasures on earth, where moth and rust destroy, and where thieves break in and steal. But store up for yourselves treasures in heaven, where moth and rust do not destroy, and where thieves do not break in and steal. For where your treasure is, there your heart will be also.

MATTHEW 6:19-21

Consider how the lilies grow. They do not labour or spin. Yet I tell you, not even Solomon in all his splendour was dressed like one of these. If that is how God clothes the grass of the field, which is here today, and tomorrow is thrown into the fire, how much more will he clothe you, O you of little faith! And do not set your heart on what you will eat or drink; do not worry about it. For the pagan world runs after such things, and your Father knows that you need them. But seek his kingdom, and these things will be given to you as well.

LUKE 12:27-31

No-one who puts his hand to the plough and looks back is fit for service in the kingdom of God.

LUKE 9:62

*T*he kingdom of heaven is like a king who prepared a wedding banquet for his son. He sent his servants to those who had been invited to the banquet to tell them to come, but they refused to come.

Then he sent some more servants and said, 'Tell those who have been invited that I have prepared my dinner: My oxen and fattened cattle have been slaughtered and everything is ready. Come to the wedding banquet.

But they paid no attention and went off – one to his field, another to his business. The rest seized his servants, ill-treated them and killed them. The king was enraged. He sent his army and destroyed those murderers and burned their city.

Then he said to his servants, 'The wedding banquet is ready, but those I invited did not deserve to come. Go to the street corners and invite to the banquet anyone you find.' So the servants went out into the streets and gathered all the people they could find, both good and bad, and the wedding hall was filled with guests.

MATTHEW 22:2-10

*N*o-one who has left home or wife or brothers or parents or children for the sake of the kingdom of God will fail to receive many times as much in this age and, in the age to come, eternal life.

LUKE 18:29-30

*T*he good news of the kingdom of God is being preached, and everyone is forcing his way into it. It is easier for heaven and earth to disappear than for the least stroke of a pen to drop out of the Law.

LUKE 16:16-17

*W*hen you enter a town and are welcomed, eat what is set before you. Heal the sick who are there and tell them, 'The kingdom of God is near you.'

LUKE 10:8-9

*A*ny kingdom divided against itself will be ruined, and a house divided against itself will fall. If Satan is divided against himself, how can his kingdom stand? I say this because you claim that I drive out demons by Beelzebub. Now if I drive out demons by Beelzebub, by whom do your followers drive them out? So then, they will be your judges. But if I drive out demons by the finger of God, then the kingdom of God has come to you.

LUKE 11:17-20

*T*he kingdom of God does not come with your careful observation, nor will people say, 'Here it is,' or 'There it is,' because the kingdom of God is within you.

LUKE 17:20-1

*L*ook at the fig-tree and all the trees. When they sprout leaves, you can see for yourselves and know that summer is near. Even so, when you see these things happening, you know that the kingdom of God is near.

LUKE 21:30-1

*B*e on guard! Be alert! You do not know when that time will come. It's like a man going away: He leaves his house and puts his servants in charge, each with his assigned task, and tells the one at the door to keep watch.

Therefore keep watch because you do not know when the owner of the house will come back – whether in the evening, or at midnight, or when the cock crows, or at dawn. If he comes suddenly, do not let him find you sleeping. What I say to you, I say to everyone: 'Watch!'

MARK 13:33-7

$\mathcal{B}$e careful, or your hearts will be weighed down with dissipation, drunkenness and the anxieties of life, and that day will close on you unexpectedly like a trap. For it will come upon all those who live on the face of the whole earth. Be always on the watch, and pray that you may be able to escape all that is about to happen, and that you may be able to stand before the Son of Man.

LUKE 21:34-6

$\mathcal{N}$o-one knows about that day or hour, not even the angels in heaven, nor the Son, but only the Father. As it was in the days of Noah, so it will be at the coming of the Son of Man. For in the days before the flood, people were eating and drinking, marrying and giving in marriage, up to the day Noah entered the ark, and they knew nothing about what would happen until the flood came and took them away. That is how it will be at the coming of the Son of Man. Two men will be in the field; one will be taken and the other left. Two women will be grinding with a hand mill; one will be taken and the other left.

MATTHEW 24:36-41

*W*hat shall we say the kingdom of God is like, or what parable shall we use to describe it? It is like a mustard seed, which is the smallest seed you plant in the ground. Yet when planted, it grows and becomes the largest of all garden plants, with such big branches that the birds of the air can perch in its shade.

MARK 4:30-3

*W*hat shall I compare the kingdom of God to? It is like yeast that a woman took and mixed into a large amount of flour until it worked all through the dough.

LUKE 13:20-1

*T*he kingdom of heaven will be like ten virgins who took their lamps and went out to meet the bridegroom. Five of them were foolish and five were wise. The foolish ones took their lamps but did not take any oil with them. The wise, however, took oil in jars along with their lamps. The bridegroom was a long time in coming, and they all became drowsy and fell asleep.

At midnight a cry rang out: 'Here's the bridegroom! Come out to meet him!'

Then all the virgins woke up and trimmed their lamps. The foolish ones said to the wise, 'Give us some of your oil; our lamps are going out.'

'No,' they replied, 'there may not be enough for both us and you. Instead, go to those who sell oil and buy some for yourselves.'

But while they were on their way to buy the oil, the bridegroom arrived. The virgins who were ready went in with him to the wedding banquet. And the door was shut.

Later the others also came. 'Sir! Sir!' they said. 'Open the door for us!'

But he replied, 'I tell you the truth, I don't know you.'

Therefore keep watch, because you do not know the day or the hour.

MATTHEW 25:1-13

*W*ho then is the faithful and wise manager, whom the master puts in charge of his servants to give them their food allowance at the proper time? It will be good for that servant whom the master finds doing so when he returns. I tell you the truth, he will put him in charge of his possessions. But suppose the servant says to himself, 'My master is taking a long time in coming,' and he then begins to beat the menservants and maidservants and to eat and drink and get drunk. The master of that servant will come on a day when he does not expect him and at an hour he is not aware of. He will cut him to pieces and assign him a place with the unbelievers.

That servant who knows his master's will and does not get ready or does not do what his master wants will be beaten with many blows. But the one who does not know and does things deserving punishment will be beaten with a few blows. From everyone who has been given much, much will be demanded; and from the one who has been entrusted with much, much more will be asked.

LUKE 12:42-8

*T*he kingdom of heaven is like a landowner who went out early in the morning to hire men to work in his vineyard. He agreed to pay them a denarius for the day and sent them into his vineyard.

About the third hour he went out and saw others standing in the market-place doing nothing. He told them, 'You also go and work in my vineyard, and I will pay you whatever is right.' So they went.

He went out again about the sixth hour and the ninth hour and did the same thing. About the eleventh hour he went out and found still others standing around. He asked them, 'Why have you been standing here all day long doing nothing?'

'Because no-one has hired us,' they answered.

He said to them, 'You also go and work in my vineyard.'

When evening came, the owner of the vineyard said to his foreman, 'Call the workers and pay them their wages, beginning with the last ones hired and going on to the first' …

MATTHEW 20:1-8

... *T*he workers who were hired about the eleventh hour came and each received a denarius. So when those came who were hired first, they expected to receive more. But each one of them also received a denarius. When they received it, they began to grumble against the landowner. 'These men who were hired last worked only one hour,' they said, 'and you have made them equal to us who have borne the burden of the work and the heat of the day.'

But he answered one of them, 'Friend, I am not being unfair to you. Didn't you agree to work for a denarius? Take your pay and go. I want to give the man who was hired last the same as I gave you. Don't I have the right to do what I want with my own money? Or are you envious because I am generous?'

So the last will be first, and the first will be last.

MATTHEW 20:9-16

*The disciples came to Jesus and asked, 'Who is the greatest
in the kingdom of heaven?'*

*He called a little child and had him stand among
them ...*

... *U*nless you change and become like little children, you will never enter the kingdom of heaven.
Therefore, whoever humbles himself like this child is
the greatest in the kingdom of heaven.

MATTHEW 18:3-4

*Y*ou are Peter, and on this rock I will build my
church, and the gates of Hades will not overcome it. I
will give you the keys of the kingdom of heaven; whatever you bind on earth will be bound in heaven and
whatever you loose on earth will be loosed in heaven.

MATTHEW 16:18-19

Then he took the cup, gave thanks and offered it to them ...

... *I* will not drink of this fruit of the vine from now on until that day when I drink it anew in my Father's kingdom.

MATTHEW 26:29

$\mathcal{B}$lessed are the poor in spirit,
  for theirs is the kingdom of heaven.
Blessed are those who mourn,
  for they will be comforted.
Blessed are the meek,
  for they will inherit the earth.
Blessed are those who hunger and thirst for
    righteousness,
  for they will be filled.
Blessed are the merciful,
  for they will be shown mercy.
Blessed are the pure in heart,
  for they will see God.
Blessed are the peacemakers,
  for they will be called sons of God.
Blessed are those who are persecuted because of
    righteousness,
  for theirs is the kingdom of heaven.

MATTHEW 5:3-10

*N*o-one can see the kingdom of God unless he is born again ... no-one can enter the kingdom of God unless he is born of water and the Spirit.

JOHN 3:3,5

I am with you for only a short time, and then I go to the one who sent me. You will look for me, but you will not find me; and where I am, you cannot come.

JOHN 7:33-4

Jesus said [to Pilate],

*M*y kingdom is not of this world. If it were, my servants would fight to prevent my arrest by the Jews. But now my kingdom is from another place.

JOHN 18:36

57

THY WILL BE DONE ON EARTH AS IT IS IN HEAVEN

Come to me, all you who are weary and burdened, and I will give you rest. Take my yoke upon you and learn from me, for I am gentle and humble in heart, and you will find rest for your souls. For my yoke is easy and my burden is light.

MATTHEW 11:28-30

*T*here was a man who had two sons. He went to the first and said, 'Son, go and work today in the vineyard.'

'I will not,' he answered, but later he changed his mind and went.

Then the father went to the other son and said the same thing. He answered, 'I will, sir,' but he did not go.

Which of the two did what his father wanted?

MATTHEW 21:28-31

*F*rom the days of John the Baptist until now, the kingdom of heaven has been forcefully advancing, and forceful men lay hold of it.

MATTHEW 11:12

*D*o not think that I have come to abolish the Law or the Prophets; I have not come to abolish them but to fulfil them. I tell you the truth, until heaven and earth disappear, not the smallest letter, not the least stroke of a pen, will by any means disappear from the Law until everything is accomplished.

MATTHEW 5:17-18

I tell you the truth, whatever you bind on earth will be bound in heaven and whatever you loose on earth will be loosed in heaven.

MATTHEW 18:18

Jesus' mother and brothers arrived. Standing outside they sent someone in to call him. A crowd was sitting around him, and they told him, 'Your mother and brothers are outside looking for you.'

*W*ho are my mother and my brothers? ... Here are my mother and my brothers! Whoever does God's will is my brother and sister and mother.

MARK 3:33-5

*Y*ou have heard that it was said to the people long ago, 'Do not murder, and anyone who murders will be subject to judgment.' But I tell you that anyone who is angry with his brother will be subject to judgment. Again, anyone who says to his brother, 'Raca,' is answerable to the Sanhedrin. But anyone who says, 'You fool!' will be in danger of the fire of hell.

MATTHEW 5:21-2

*W*hen you give a luncheon or dinner, do not invite your friends, your brothers or relatives, or your rich neighbours; if you do, they may invite you back and so you will be repaid. But when you give a banquet, invite the poor, the crippled, the lame, the blind, and you will be blessed. Although they cannot repay you, you will be repaid at the resurrection of the righteous.

LUKE 14:12-14

𝒜 man was going down from Jerusalem to Jericho, when he fell into the hands of robbers. They stripped him of his clothes, beat him and went away, leaving him half-dead. A priest happened to be going down the same road, and when he saw the man, he passed by on the other side. So too, a Levite, when he came to the place and saw him, passed by on the other side. But a Samaritan, as he travelled, came where the man was; and when he saw him, he took pity on him. He went to him and bandaged his wounds, pouring on oil and wine. Then he put the man on his own donkey, brought him to an inn and took care of him. The next day he took out two silver coins and gave them to the innkeeper. 'Look after him,' he said, 'and when I return, I will reimburse you for any extra expense you may have.'

Which of these three do you think was a neighbour to the man who fell into the hands of robbers?

LUKE 10:30-6

*A*nyone who divorces his wife and marries another woman commits adultery, and the man who marries a divorced woman commits adultery.

LUKE 16:18

*S*uppose one of you had a servant ploughing or looking after the sheep. Would he say to the servant when he comes in from the field, 'Come along now and sit down to eat?' Would he not rather say, 'Prepare my supper, get yourself ready and wait on me while I eat and drink; after that you may eat and drink'? Would he thank the servant because he did what he was told to do? So you also, when you have done everything you were told to do, should say, 'We are unworthy servants; we have only done our duty.'

LUKE 17:7-10

*A [Roman] centurion's servant, whom his master valued
highly, was sick and about to die. The centurion heard of
Jesus and sent some elders of the Jews to him ... [Jesus]
was not far from the house when the centurion sent friends
to say to him: 'Lord, don't trouble yourself, for I do not
deserve to have you come under my roof. That is why I did
not even consider myself worthy to come to you. But say
the word and my servant will be healed ...'*

I tell you, I have not found such great faith even in
Israel.

LUKE 7:9

*W*hoever finds his life will lose it, and whoever
loses his life for my sake will find it.

MATTHEW 10:39

A certain man was preparing a great banquet and invited many guests. At the time of the banquet he sent his servant to tell those who had been invited, 'Come, for everything is now ready.'

But they all alike began to make excuses. The first said, 'I have just bought a field, and I must go and see it. Please excuse me.'

Another said, 'I have just bought five yoke of oxen, and I'm on my way to try them out. Please excuse me.'

Still another said, 'I have just got married, so I can't come.'

The servant came back and reported this to his master. Then the owner of the house became angry and ordered his servant, 'Go out quickly into the streets and alleys of the town and bring in the poor, the crippled, the blind and the lame.'

'Sir,' the servant said, 'what you ordered has been done, but there is still room.'

Then the master told his servant, 'Go out to the roads and country lanes and make them come in, so that my house will be full. I tell you, not one of those men who were invited will get a taste of my banquet.'

LUKE 14:16-24

The most important [commandment] is this:

'*H*ear, O Israel, the Lord our God, the Lord is one. Love the Lord your God with all your heart and with all your soul and with all your mind and with all your strength.' The second is this: 'Love your neighbour as yourself.' There is no commandment greater than these.

MARK 12:29-31

*T*he good man brings good things out of the good stored up in his heart, and the evil man brings evil things out of the evil stored up in his heart. For out of the overflow of his heart his mouth speaks.

LUKE 6:45

The Pharisees and teachers of the law asked Jesus, 'Why don't your disciples live according to the tradition of the elders instead of eating their food with "unclean" hands?'

Isaiah was right when he prophesied about you hypocrites; as it is written:

> These people honour me with their lips,
>   but their hearts are far from me.
> They worship me in vain;
>   their teachings are but rules taught by men.

You have let go of the commands of God and are holding on to the traditions of men.

MARK 7:6-8

*Y*ou have a fine way of setting aside the commands
of God in order to observe your own traditions! For
Moses said, 'Honour your father and your mother,' and,
'Anyone who curses his father or mother must be put
to death.' But you say that if a man says to his father or
mother: 'Whatever help you might otherwise have received from me is Corban' (*that is, a gift devoted to
God*), then you no longer let him do anything for his
father or mother. Thus you nullify the word of God by
your tradition that you have handed down. And you
do many things like that.

MARK 7:9-13

*D*on't you see that nothing that enters a man from the outside can make him 'unclean'? For it doesn't go into his heart but into his stomach, and then out of his body. (*In saying this, Jesus declared all foods 'clean'*) …

What comes out of a man is what makes him 'unclean'. For from within, out of men's hearts, come evil thoughts, sexual immorality, theft, murder, adultery, malice, deceit, lewdness, envy, slander, arrogance and folly. All these evils come from inside and make a man 'unclean'.

MARK 7:18-23

*N*ot everyone who says to me, 'Lord, Lord,' will enter the kingdom of heaven, but only he who does the will of my Father who is in heaven. Many will say to me on that day, 'Lord, Lord, did we not prophesy in your name, and in your name drive out demons and perform many miracles?' Then I will tell them plainly, 'I never knew you. Away from me, you evildoers!'

MATTHEW 7:21-3

*M*y food ... is to do the will of him who sent me and to finish his work.

JOHN 4:34

*B*y myself I can do nothing; I judge only as I hear, and my judgment is just, for I seek not to please myself but him who sent me.

JOHN 5:30

*M*y teaching is not my own. It comes from him who sent me. If anyone chooses to do God's will, he will find out whether my teaching comes from God or whether I speak on my own. He who speaks on his own does so to gain honour for himself, but he who works for the honour of the one who sent him is a man of truth; there is nothing false about him.

JOHN 7:16-18

*I*f you hold to my teaching, you are really my disciples. Then you will know the truth, and the truth will set you free.

JOHN 8:31-2

*T*he Father who sent me commanded me what to say and how to say it. I know that his command leads to eternal life. So whatever I say is just what the Father has told me to say.

JOHN 12:49-50

[Jesus] began to wash his disciples' feet, drying them with the towel ... He came to Simon Peter who said to him ... 'You shall never wash my feet.'

Jesus answered, 'Unless I wash you, you have no part with me.'

'Then, Lord ... not just my feet but my hands and my head as well!'

A person who has had a bath needs only to wash his feet; his whole body is clean. And you are clean, though not every one of you.

JOHN 13:10

*D*o you understand what I have done for you? You call me 'Teacher' and 'Lord', and rightly so, for that is what I am. Now that I, your Lord and Teacher, have washed your feet, you also should wash one another's feet. I have set you an example that you should do as I have done for you. I tell you the truth, no servant is greater than his master, nor is a messenger greater than the one who sent him. Now that you know these things, you will be blessed if you do them.

JOHN 13:12-17

A new command I give you: Love one another. As I have loved you, so you must love one another. By this all men will know that you are my disciples, if you love one another.

JOHN 13:34

*I*f you love me, you will obey what I command. And I will ask the Father, and he will give you another Counsellor to be with you for ever – the Spirit of truth. The world cannot accept him, because it neither sees him nor knows him. But you know him, for he lives with you and will be in you. I will not leave you as orphans; I will come to you. Before long, the world will not see me any more, but you will see me. Because I live, you also will live. On that day you will realise that I am in my Father, and you are in me, and I am in you. Whoever has my commands and obeys them, he is the one who loves me. He who loves me will be loved by my Father, and I too will love him and show myself to him.

JOHN 14:15-21

Give Us This Day Our Daily Bread

Man does not live on bread alone, but on every word that comes from the mouth of God.

MATTHEW 4:4

*A*sk and it will be given to you; seek and you will find; knock and the door will be opened to you. For everyone who asks receives; he who seeks finds; and to him who knocks, the door will be opened.

MATTHEW 7:7-8

*W*hich of you, if his son asks for bread, will give him a stone? Or if he asks for a fish, will give him a snake? If you, then, though you are evil, know how to give good gifts to your children, how much more will your Father in heaven give good gifts to those who ask him!

MATTHEW 7:9-11

*N*o-one pours new wine into old wineskins. If he does, the new wine will burst the skins, the wine will run out and the wineskins will be ruined. No, new wine must be poured into new wineskins. And no-one after drinking old wine wants the new, for he says, 'The old is better.'

LUKE 5:37-9

One Sabbath Jesus was going through the cornfields, and as his disciples walked along, they began to pick some ears of corn. The Pharisees said to him, 'Look, why are they doing what is unlawful on the Sabbath?'

*H*ave you never read what David did when he and his companions were hungry and in need? In the days of Abiathar the high priest, he entered the house of God and ate the consecrated bread which is lawful only for the priests to eat. And he also gave some to his companions … The Sabbath was made for man, not man for the Sabbath. So the Son of Man is Lord even of the Sabbath.

MARK 2:25-8

*D*o not worry about your life, what you will eat; or about your body, what you will wear. Life is more than food, and the body more than clothes. Consider the ravens: They do not sow or reap, they have no store-room or barn; yet God feeds them. And how much more valuable you are than birds! Who of you by worrying can add a single hour to his life? Since you cannot do this very little thing, why do you worry about the rest?

LUKE 12:22-6

When they went across the lake, the disciples forgot to take bread. Jesus said to them, 'Be careful … Be on your guard against the yeast of the Pharisees and Sadducees.'

They discussed this among themselves and said, 'It is because we didn't bring any bread.'

… *Y*ou of little faith, why are you talking among yourselves about having no bread? Do you still not understand? Don't you remember the five loaves for the five thousand, and how many basketfuls you gathered? … How is it you don't understand that I was not talking to you about bread? But be on your guard against the yeast of the Pharisees and Sadducees.

Then they understood that he was not telling them to guard against the yeast used in bread, but against the teaching of the Pharisees and Sadducees.

MATTHEW 16:8-11

GIVE US THIS DAY ...

A Canaanite woman ... came to him, crying out ... 'My daughter is suffering terribly from demon possession.'

I was sent only to the lost sheep of Israel ... It is not right to take the children's bread and toss it to their dogs.

'Yes, Lord,' she said, 'but even the dogs eat the crumbs that fall from their master's table' ...

Woman, you have great faith! Your request is granted.

MATTHEW 15:24-8

Suppose one of you has a friend, and he goes to him at midnight and says, 'Friend, lend me three loaves of bread, because a friend of mine on a journey has come to me, and I have nothing to set before him.'

Then the one inside answers, 'Don't bother me. The door is already locked, and my children are with me in bed. I can't get up and give you anything.' I tell you, though he will not get up and give him the bread because he is his friend, yet because of the man's bold-ness he will get up and give him as much as he needs.

LUKE 11:5-8

I have eagerly desired to eat this Passover with you before I suffer. For I tell you, I will not eat it again until it finds fulfilment in the kingdom of God.

LUKE 22:15-16

He took bread, gave thanks and broke it, and gave it to them ...

This is my body given for you; do this in remembrance of me.

LUKE 22:19

He took the cup, gave thanks and offered it to them, and they all drank from it.

This is my blood of the covenant which is poured out for many ... I will not drink again of the fruit of the vine until that day when I drink it anew in the kingdom of God.

MARK 14:24-5

A Samaritan woman came to draw water … Jesus said to her, 'Will you give me a drink?' The Samaritan woman said to him, 'You are a Jew and I am a Samaritan woman. How can you ask me for a drink?' (For Jews do not associate with Samaritans.)

… *I*f you knew the gift of God and who it is that asks you for a drink, you would have asked him and he would have given you living water.

JOHN 4:10

*Y*ou are looking for me, not because you saw miraculous signs but because you ate the loaves and had your fill. Do not work for food that spoils, but for food that endures to eternal life, which the Son of Man will give you. On him God the Father has placed his seal of approval.

JOHN 6:26-7

*I*t is not Moses who has given you the bread from heaven, but it is my Father who gives you the true bread from heaven. For the bread of God is he who comes down from heaven and gives life to the world.

JOHN 6:32-3

I am the bread of life. He who comes to me will never go hungry, and he who believes in me will never be thirsty. But as I told you, you have seen me and still you do not believe. All that the Father gives me will come to me, and whoever comes to me I will never drive away. For I have come down from heaven not to do my will but to do the will of him who sent me. And this is the will of him who sent me, that I shall lose none of all that he has given me, but raise them up at the last day. For my Father's will is that everyone who looks to the Son and believes in him shall have eternal life, and I will raise him up at the last day.

JOHN 6:35-40

I am the bread that came down from heaven.

JOHN 6:41

I am the bread of life. Your forefathers ate the manna in the desert, yet they died. But here is the bread that comes down from heaven, which a man may eat and not die. I am the living bread that came down from heaven. If anyone eats of this bread, he will live for ever. This bread is my flesh, which I will give for the life of the world.

JOHN 6:48-51

I tell you the truth, unless you can eat the flesh of the Son of Man and drink his blood, you have no life in you. Whoever eats my flesh and drinks my blood has eternal life, and I will raise him up at the last day. For my flesh is real food and my blood is real drink. Whoever eats my flesh and drinks my blood remains in me, and I in him. Just as the living Father sent me and I live because of the Father, so the one who feeds on me will live because of me. This is the bread that came down from heaven.

JOHN 6:53-8

*I*f anyone is thirsty, let him come to me and drink. Whoever believes in me, as the Scripture has said, streams of living water will flow from within him.

JOHN 7:37-8

*M*y Father will give you whatever you ask in my name. Until now you have not asked for anything in my name. Ask and you will receive, and your joy will be complete.

JOHN 16:23-4

FORGIVE US OUR TRESPASSES AS WE FORGIVE THOSE THAT TRESPASS AGAINST US

Love your enemies, do good to those who hate you, bless those who curse you, pray for those who ill-treat you. If someone strikes you on one cheek, turn to him the other also. If someone takes your cloak, do not stop him from taking your tunic. Give to everyone who asks you, and if anyone takes what belongs to you, do not demand it back. Do to others as you would have them do to you.

LUKE 6:27-31

Settle matters quickly with your adversary who is taking you to court. Do it while you are still with him on the way, or he may hand you over to the judge, and the judge may hand you over to the officer, and you may be thrown into prison. I tell you the truth, you will not get out until you have paid the last penny.

MATTHEW 5:25-6

If you forgive men when they sin against you, your heavenly Father will also forgive you. But if you do not forgive men their sins, your Father will not forgive your sins.

MATTHEW 6:14-15

Be merciful, just as your Father is merciful.

LUKE 6:36

*D*o not judge, and you will not be judged. Do not condemn, and you will not be condemned. Forgive, and you will be forgiven. Give, and it will be given to you. A good measure, pressed down, shaken together and running over, will be poured into your lap. For with the measure you use, it will be measured to you.

LUKE 6:37-8

A woman who had lived a sinful life ... learned that Jesus was eating at [Simon] the Pharisee's house ... she began to wet his feet with her tears. Then she wiped them with her hair, kissed them and poured perfume on them ...

Simon, I have something to tell you ... Two men owed money to a certain money-lender. One owed him five hundred denarii, and the other fifty. Neither of them had the money to pay him back, so he cancelled the debts of both. Now which of them will love him more?

... 'I suppose the one who had the bigger debt cancelled.'

You have judged correctly ... Do you see this woman? I came into your house. You did not give me water for my feet, but she wet my feet with her tears and wiped them with her hair. You did not give me a kiss, but this woman, from the time I entered, has not stopped kissing my feet. You did not put oil on my head, but she has poured perfume on my feet. Therefore, I tell you, her many sins have been forgiven – for she loved much. But he who has been forgiven little loves little.

LUKE 7:40-7

97

*Y*ou have heard that it was said, 'Love your neighbour and hate your enemy. But I tell you: Love your enemies and pray for those who persecute you, that you may be sons of your Father in heaven. He causes his sun to rise on the evil and the good, and sends rain on the righteous and the unrighteous. If you love those who love you, what reward will you get? Are not even the tax collectors doing that? And if you greet only your brothers, what are you doing more than others? Do not even pagans do that? Be perfect, therefore, as your heavenly Father is perfect.

MATTHEW 5:43-8

*I*f you are offering your gift at the altar and there remember that your brother has something against you, leave your gift there in front of the altar. First go and be reconciled to your brother; then come and offer your gift.

MATTHEW 5:23-4

*I*t is not the healthy who need a doctor, but the sick. But go and learn what this means: 'I desire mercy, not sacrifice.' For I have not come to call the righteous, but sinners.

MATTHEW 9:12-13

*I*f your brother sins against you, go and show him his fault, just between the two of you. If he listens to you, you have won your brother over. But if he will not listen, take one or two others along, so that 'every matter may be established by the testimony of two or three witnesses'. If he refuses to listen to them, tell it to the church; and if he refuses to listen even to the church, treat him as you would a pagan or a tax collector.

MATTHEW 18:15-17

*I*f anyone says to this mountain, 'Go, throw yourself into the sea,' and does not doubt in his heart but believes that what he says will happen, it will be done for him. Therefore I tell you, whatever you ask for in prayer, believe that you have received it, and it will be yours. And when you stand praying, if you hold anything against anyone, forgive him, so that your Father in heaven may forgive you your sins.

MARK 11:23-6

*T*he kingdom of heaven is like a king who wanted to settle accounts with his servants. As he began the settlement, a man who owed him ten thousand talents was brought to him. Since he was not able to pay, the master ordered that he and his wife and his children and all that he had be sold to repay the debt.

The servant fell on his knees before him. 'Be patient with me,' he begged, 'and I will pay back everything.' The servant's master took pity on him, cancelled the debt and let him go.

But when that servant went out, he found one of his fellow-servants who owed him a hundred denarii. He grabbed him and began to choke him. 'Pay back what you owe me!' he demanded.

His fellow-servant fell to his knees and begged him, 'Be patient with me, and I will pay you back.'

But he refused. Instead, he went off and had the man thrown into prison until he could pay the debt. When the other servants saw what had happened, they were greatly distressed and went and told their master everything that had happened …

MATTHEW 18:23-31

... *T*he master called the servant in. 'You wicked servant,' he said, 'I cancelled all that debt of yours because you begged me to. Shouldn't you have had mercy
on your fellow-servant just as I had on you?' In anger
his master turned him over to the jailers to be tortured,
until he should pay back all he owed.

This is how my heavenly Father will treat each of
you unless you forgive your brother from your heart.

MATTHEW 18:32-5

*I*f your brother sins, rebuke him, and if he repents,
forgive him. If he sins against you seven times in a day,
and seven times comes back to you and says, 'I repent,'
forgive him.

LUKE 17:3-4

The teachers of the law and the Pharisees ... said to Jesus,
'Teacher, this woman was caught in the act of adultery. In
the Law Moses commanded us to stone such women. Now
what do you say?' ...

If any one of you is without sin, let him be the first to
throw a stone at her.

JOHN 8:8

Receive the Holy Spirit. If you forgive anyone his
sins, they are forgiven; if you do not forgive them, they
are not forgiven.

JOHN 20:22-3

LEAD US NOT INTO TEMPTATION

*Do not let your hearts be troubled.
Trust in God; trust also in me. In my
Father's house are many rooms; if it
were not so, I would have told you.
I am going there to prepare a place for you.
And if I go and prepare a place for you,
I will come back and take you
to be with me that you also
may be where I am.
You know the way to the place
where I am going.*

JOHN 14:1-4

*I*f anyone causes one of these little ones who believe in me to sin, it would be better for him to have a large millstone hung around his neck and to be drowned in the depths of the sea.

MATTHEW 18:6

$\mathcal{N}$ation will rise against nation, and kingdom against kingdom. There will be great earthquakes, famines and pestilences in various places, and fearful events and great signs from heaven.

But before all this, they will lay hands on you and persecute you. They will deliver you to synagogues and prisons and you will be brought before kings and governors, and all on account of my name. This will result in your being witnesses to them. But make up your mind not to worry beforehand how you will defend yourselves. For I will give you words and wisdom that none of your adversaries will be able to resist or contradict. You will be betrayed even by parents, brothers, relatives and friends, and they will put some of you to death. All men will hate you because of me. But not a hair of your head will perish. By standing firm you will gain life.

LUKE 21:10-19

I am sending you out like sheep among wolves. Therefore be as shrewd as snakes and as innocent as doves.

MATTHEW 10:16

*T*he Son of Man must suffer many things and be rejected by the elders, chief priests and teachers of the law, and he must be killed and on the third day be raised to life.

LUKE 9:22

*W*hoever acknowledges me before men, the Son of Man will also acknowledge him before the angels of God. But he who disowns me before men will be disowned before the angels of God.

LUKE 12:8-9

*T*he ground of a certain rich man produced a good crop. He thought to himself, 'What shall I do? I have no place to store my crops.'

Then he said, 'This is what I'll do. I will tear down my barns and build bigger ones, and there I will store all my grain and my goods. And I'll say to myself, "You have plenty of good things laid up for many years. Take life easy; eat, drink and be merry." '

But God said to him, 'You fool! This very night your life will be demanded from you. Then who will get what you have prepared for yourself?'

This is how it will be with anyone who stores up things for himself but is not rich towards God.

LUKE 12:16-21

*E*veryone who hears these words of mine and puts them into practice is like a wise man who built his house on the rock. The rain came down, the streams rose, and the winds blew and beat against that house; yet it did not fall, because it had its foundation on the rock. But everyone who hears these words of mine and does not put them into practice is like a foolish man who built his house on sand. The rain came down, the streams rose, and the winds blew and beat against that house, and it fell with a great crash.

MATTHEW 7:24-7

*D*o not be afraid of those who kill the body and after that can do no more. But I will show you whom you should fear: Fear him who, after the killing of the body, has power to throw you into hell. Yes, I tell you, fear him. Are not five sparrows sold for two pennies? Yet not one of them is forgotten by God. Indeed, the very hairs of your head are all numbered. Don't be afraid; you are worth more than many sparrows.

LUKE 12:4-7

*Y*ou have heard that it was said, 'Do not commit adultery.' But I tell you that anyone who looks at a woman lustfully has already committed adultery with her in his heart. If your right eye causes you to sin, gouge it out and throw it away. It is better for you to lose one part of your body than for your whole body to be thrown into hell. And if your right hand causes you to sin, cut it off and throw it away. It is better for you to lose one part of your body than for your whole body to go into hell.

MATTHEW 5:27-30

*D*o not suppose that I have come to bring peace to the earth. I did not come to bring peace, but a sword. For I have come to turn

'a man against his father,
a daughter against her mother,
a daughter-in-law against her mother-in-law –
a man's enemies will be the members of his own
     household.'

MATTHEW 10:34-6

They went to a place called Gethsemane ... [Jesus] took Peter, James and John along with him, and he began to be deeply distressed and troubled.

*M*y soul is overwhelmed with sorrow to the point of death ... Stay here and keep watch.

MARK 14:34

... *A*re you asleep? Could you not keep watch for one hour? Watch and pray so that you will not fall into temptation. The spirit is willing, but the body is weak.

MARK 14:37-8

Going a little further, he fell with his face to the ground, and prayed,

*M*y Father, if it is not possible for this cup to be taken way unless I drink it, may your will be done.

MATTHEW 26:42

Many of his disciples turned back and no longer followed him … Jesus asked the Twelve,

You do not want to leave too, do you?

JOHN 6:67

In this world you will have trouble. But take heart! I have overcome the world.

JOHN 16:33

Deliver Us from Evil

Be on your guard against men; they will hand you over to the local councils and flog you in their synagogues. On my account you will be brought before governors and kings as witnesses to them and to the Gentiles. But when they arrest you, do not worry about what to say or how to say it. At that time you will be given what to say, for it will not be you speaking, but the Spirit of your Father speaking through you.

MATTHEW 10:17-20

*D*o not be afraid of those who kill the body but cannot kill the soul. Rather, be afraid of the One who can destroy both soul and body in hell.

MATTHEW 10:28

*W*hen you are persecuted in one place, flee to another. I tell you the truth, you will not finish going through the cities of Israel before the Son of Man comes.

MATTHEW 10:23

*Y*ou must be on your guard. You will be handed over to the local councils and flogged in the synagogues. On account of me you will stand before governors and kings as witnesses to them. And the gospel must first be preached to all nations. Whenever you are arrested and brought to trial, do not worry beforehand about what to say. Just say whatever is given you at the time, for it is not you speaking, but the Holy Spirit.

Brother will betray brother to death, and a father his child. Children will rebel against their parents and have them put to death. All men will hate you because of me, but he who stands firm to the end will be saved.

MARK 13:9-13

*I*t is not the healthy who need a doctor, but the sick. I have not come to call the righteous, but sinners to repentance.

LUKE 5:31

Zacchaeus … was a chief tax collector and was wealthy. He wanted to see who Jesus was, but being a short man he could not, because of the crowd … He ran ahead and climbed a sycamore-fig tree to see him … When Jesus reached the spot he looked up …

*Z*acchaeus, come down immediately. I must stay at your house … Today salvation has come to this house, because this man, too, is a son of Abraham. For the Son of Man came to seek and to save what was lost.

LUKE 19:5,9

Some men … went up on the roof and lowered [a paralysed man] on his mat through the tiles into the middle of the crowd, right in front of Jesus. When Jesus saw their faith, he said,

*F*riend, your sins are forgiven …

LUKE 5:20

*W*hich is easier to say, 'Your sins are forgiven,' or to say, 'Get up and walk'? But that you may know that the Son of Man has authority on earth to forgive sins ...

He said to the paralysed man, I tell you, get up, take up your mat and go home.

LUKE 5:23-4

Two blind men followed Jesus, calling out, 'Have mercy on us, Son of David!' ...

He asked them, 'Do you believe that I am able to do this?'

'Yes, Lord,' they replied.

Then he touched their eyes.

*A*ccording to your faith will it be done to you.

MATTHEW 9:29

As Jesus was on his way, the crowds almost crushed him.
And a woman was there who had been subject to bleeding
for twelve years, but no-one could heal her. She came up
behind him and touched the edge of his cloak, and immedi-
ately her bleeding stopped.

Someone touched me; I know that power has gone
out from me ...

LUKE 8:46

... Daughter, your faith has healed you. Go in peace
and be freed from your suffering.

MARK 5:34

*W*hen an evil spirit comes out of a man, it goes
through arid places seeking rest and does not find it.
Then it says, 'I will return to the house I left.' When it
arrives, it finds the house swept clean and put in order.
Then it goes and takes seven other spirits more wicked
than itself, and they go in and live there. And the final
condition of that man is worse than the first.

LUKE 11:24-6

*T*hese signs will accompany those who believe: In my
name they will drive out demons; they will speak in
new tongues; they will pick up snakes with their
hands; and when they drink deadly poison, it will not
hurt them at all; they will place their hands on sick
people, and they will get well.

MARK 16:17-18

*B*lessed are you when people insult you, persecute you and falsely say all kinds of evil against you because of me. Rejoice and be glad, because great is your reward in heaven, for in the same way they persecuted the prophets who were before you.

MATTHEW 5:11-12

I have given you authority to trample on snakes and scorpions and to overcome all the power of the enemy; nothing will harm you. However, do not rejoice that the spirits submit to you, but rejoice that your names are written in heaven.

LUKE 10:19-20

*T*hose eighteen who died when the tower in Siloam fell on them – do you think they were more guilty than all the others living in Jerusalem? I tell you, no! But unless you repent, you too will all perish.

LUKE 13:4-5

*On a Sabbath Jesus was teaching in one of the synagogues,
and a woman was there who had been crippled by a spirit
for eighteen years. She was bent over and could not
straighten up at all. When Jesus saw her, he called her for-
ward and said to her,*

Woman, you are set free from your infirmity.

LUKE 13:12

*Indignant because Jesus had healed on the Sabbath, the
synagogue ruler said to the people, 'There are six days for
work. So come and be healed on one of those, not on the
Sabbath.' …*

You hypocrites! Doesn't each of you on the Sabbath
untie his ox or donkey from the stall and lead it out to
give it water? Then should not this woman, a daughter
of Abraham, whom Satan has kept bound for eighteen
long years, be set free on the Sabbath day from what
bound her?

LUKE 13:15-16

*T*here was a rich man who was dressed in purple and fine linen and lived in luxury every day. At his gate was laid a beggar named Lazarus, covered with sores and longing to eat what fell from the rich man's table. Even the dogs came and licked his sores.

The time came when the beggar died and the angels carried him to Abraham's side. The rich man also died and was buried. In hell, where he was in torment, he looked up and saw Abraham far away, with Lazarus by his side. So he called to him, 'Father Abraham, have pity on me and send Lazarus to dip the tip of his finger in water and cool my tongue, because I am in agony in this fire.'

But Abraham replied, 'Son, remember that in your lifetime you received your good things, while Lazarus received bad things, but now he is comforted here and you are in agony. And besides all this, between us and you a great chasm has been fixed, so that those who want to go from here to you cannot, nor can anyone cross over from there to us.'

He answered, 'Then I beg you, father, send Lazarus to my father's house, for I have five brothers. Let him warn them, so that they will not also come to this place of torment.'

Abraham replied, 'They have Moses and the

Prophets; let them listen to them.'

'No, father Abraham,' he said, 'but if someone from the dead goes to them, they will repent.'

He said to him, 'If they do not listen to Moses and the Prophets, they will not be convinced even if someone rises from the dead.'

LUKE 16:19-31

A man of noble birth went to a distant country to have himself appointed king and then to return. So he called ten of his servants and gave them ten minas. 'Put this money to work,' he said, 'until I come back.'

But his subjects hated him and sent a delegation after him to say, 'We don't want this man to be our king.'

He was made king, however, and returned home. Then he sent for the servants to whom he had given the money, in order to find out what they had gained with it …

LUKE 19:12-15

... *T*he first [servant] came and said, 'Sir, your mina has earned ten more.'

'Well done, my good servant!' his master replied. 'Because you have been trustworthy in a very small matter, take charge of ten cities.'

The second came and said, 'Sir, your mina has earned five more.'

His master answered, 'You take charge of five cities.'

Then another servant came and said, 'Sir, here is your mina; I have kept it laid away in a piece of cloth. I was afraid of you, because you are a hard man. You take out what you did not put in and reap what you did not sow.'

His master replied, 'I will judge you by your own words, you wicked servant! You knew, did you, that I am a hard man, taking out what I did not put in, and reaping what I did not sow? Why then didn't you put my money on deposit, so that when I came back, I could have collected it with interest?'

Then he said to those standing by, 'Take his mina away from him and give it to the one who has ten minas.'

'Sir,' they replied, 'he already has ten!'

He replied, 'I tell you that to every one who has, more will be given, but as for the one who has nothing, even what he has will be taken away.'

LUKE 19:16-26

*M*any will turn away from the faith and will betray and hate each other, and many false prophets will appear and deceive many people. Because of the increase of wickedness, the love of most will grow cold, but he who stands firm to the end will be saved. And this gospel of the kingdom will be preached in the whole world as a testimony to all nations, and then the end will come.

MATTHEW 24:10-14

*T*his very night you will all fall away on account of me, for it is written:

> 'I will strike the shepherd,
> and the sheep of the flock will be scattered.'

But after I have risen, I will go ahead of you into Galilee.

MATTHEW 26:31-2

*S*imon, Simon, Satan has asked to sift you as wheat. But I have prayed for you, Simon, that your faith may not fail. And when you have turned back, strengthen your brothers.

LUKE 22:31-2

*D*aughters of Jerusalem, do not weep for me; weep for yourselves and for your children. For the time will come when you will say, 'Blessed are the barren women, the wombs that never bore and the breasts that never nursed!' Then

> 'they will say to the mountains, "Fall on us!"
> and to the hills "Cover us!" '

For if men do these things when the tree is green, what will happen when it is dry?

LUKE 23:28-31

*T*he man who does not enter the sheep pen by the gate, but climbs in by some other way, is a thief and a robber. The man who enters by the gate is the shepherd of his sheep. The watchman opens the gate for him, and the sheep listen to his voice. He calls his own sheep by name and leads them out. When he has brought out all his own, he goes on ahead of them, and his sheep follow him because they know his voice. But they will never follow a stranger; in fact, they will run away from him because they do not recognise a stranger's voice.

JOHN 10:1-5

[Simon] Peter asked, 'Lord, why can't I follow you now? I will lay down my life for you.'

*W*ill you really lay down your life for me? I tell you the truth, before the cock crows, you will disown me three times!

JOHN 13:38

I am coming to you now, but I say these things while I am still in the world, so that they may have the full measure of my joy within them. I have given them your word and the world has hated them, for they are not of the world any more than I am of the world. My prayer is not that you take them out of the world but that you protect them from the evil one. They are not of the world, even as I am not of it. Sanctify them by the truth; your word is truth. As you sent me into the world, I have sent them into the world. For them I sanctify myself, that they too may be truly sanctified.

JOHN 17:13-19

*F*OR THINE IS THE

KINGDOM, THE POWER AND

THE GLORY

You are those who have stood by me in my trials.
And I confer on you a kingdom, just as my Father
conferred one on me, so that you may eat and drink
at my table in my kingdom and sit on thrones,
judging the twelve tribes of Israel.

LUKE 22:28-30

*D*o not be afraid, little flock, for your Father has been pleased to give you the kingdom. Sell your possessions and give to the poor. Provide purses for yourselves that will not wear out, a treasure in heaven that will not be exhausted, where no thief comes near and no moth destroys. For where your treasure is, there your heart will be also.

LUKE 12:32-4

*T*wo men went up to the temple to pray, one a Pharisee and the other a tax collector. The Pharisee stood up and prayed about himself: 'God, I thank you that I am not like other men – robbers, evildoers, adulterers – or even like this tax collector. I fast twice a week and give a tenth of all I get.'

But the tax collector stood at a distance. He would not even look up to heaven, but beat his breast and said, 'God, have mercy on me, a sinner.'

I tell you that this man, rather than the other, went home justified before God. For everyone who exalts himself will be humbled, and he who humbles himself will be exalted.

LUKE 18:10-14

*C*hildren, how hard it is to enter the kingdom of God! It is easier for a camel to go through the eye of a needle than for a rich man to enter the kingdom of God.

MARK 10:24-5

*Y*ou do not know the Scriptures or the power of God. At the resurrection people will neither marry nor be given in marriage; they will be like the angels in heaven. But about the resurrection of the dead – have you not read what God said to you, 'I am the God of Abraham, the God of Isaac, and the God of Jacob'? He is not the God of the dead but of the living.

MATTHEW 22:29-32

*P*eople will come from east and west and north and south, and will take their places at the feast in the kingdom of God. Indeed there are those who are last who will be first, and first who will be last.

LUKE 13:29-30

137

*W*hen the Son of Man comes in his glory, and all the angels with him, he will sit on his throne in heavenly glory. All the nations will be gathered before him, and he will separate the people one from another as a shepherd separates the sheep from the goats. He will put the sheep on his right and the goats on his left.

Then the King will say to those on his right, 'Come, you who are blessed by my Father; take your inheritance, the kingdom prepared for you since the creation of the world. For I was hungry and you gave me something to eat, I was thirsty and you gave me something to drink, I was a stranger and you invited me in, I needed clothes and you clothed me, I was sick and you looked after me, I was in prison and you came to visit me.'

Then the righteous will answer him, 'Lord, when did we see you hungry and feed you, or thirsty and give you something to drink? When did we see you a stranger and invite you in, or needing clothes and clothe you? When did we see you sick or in prison and go to visit you?'

The King will reply, 'I tell you the truth, whatever you did for one of the least of these brothers of mine, you did for me.'

MATTHEW 25:31-40

*A*ll authority in heaven and on earth has been given to me. Therefore go and make disciples of all nations, baptising them in the name of the Father and of the Son and of the Holy Spirit, and teaching them to obey everything I have commanded you. And surely I am with you always, to the very end of the age.

MATTHEW 28:18-20

*T*here will be signs in the sun, moon and stars. On the earth, nations will be in anguish and perplexity at the roaring and tossing of the sea. Men will faint from terror, apprehensive of what is coming on the world, for the heavenly bodies will be shaken. At that time they will see the Son of Man coming in a cloud with power and great glory. When these things begin to take place, stand up and lift up your heads, because your redemption is drawing near.

LUKE 21:25-8

*N*o-one knows about that day or hour, not even the angels in heaven, nor the Son, but only the Father.

MARK 13:32

*H*eaven and earth will pass away, but my words will never pass away.

MARK 13:31

O Jerusalem, Jerusalem, you who kill the prophets and stone those sent to you, how often I have longed to gather your children together, as a hen gathers her chicks under her wings, but you were not willing. Look, your house is left to you desolate. For I tell you, you will not see me again until you say, 'Blessed is he who comes in the name of the Lord.'

MATTHEW 23:37-9

I tell you the truth, at the renewal of all things, when the Son of Man sits on his glorious throne, you who have followed me will also sit on twelve thrones, judging the twelve tribes of Israel. And everyone who has left houses or brothers or sisters or father or mother or children or fields for my sake will receive a hundred times as much and will inherit eternal life. But many who are first will be last, and many who are last will be first.

MATTHEW 19:28-30

*I*n a certain town there was a judge who neither feared God nor cared about men. And there was a widow in that town who kept coming to him with the plea, 'Grant me justice against my adversary.'

For some time he refused. But finally he said to himself, 'Even though I don't fear God or care about men, yet because this widow keeps bothering me, I will see that she gets justice, so that she won't eventually wear me out with her coming!' …

Listen to what the judge says. And will not God bring about justice for his chosen ones, who cry out to him day and night? Will he keep putting them off? I tell you, he will see that they get justice, and quickly. However, when the Son of Man comes, will he find faith on the earth?

LUKE 18:2-8

The high priest asked him, 'Are you the Christ, the Son of the Blessed One?'

I am. And you will see the Son of Man sitting at the right hand of the Mighty One and coming on the clouds of heaven.

MARK 14:62

Two other men, both criminals, were also led out with Jesus to be crucified. One of the criminals said, 'Jesus, remember me when you come into your kingdom.'

I tell you the truth, today you will be with me in paradise.

LUKE 23:43

Two of them were going to a village called Emmaus …
Jesus himself came up and walked along with them; but
they were kept from recognising him …

*H*ow foolish you are, and how slow of heart to
believe all that the prophets have spoken! Did not the
Christ have to suffer these things and then enter his
glory?

LUKE 24:25-6

After his suffering, [Jesus] showed himself to the [apostles]
and gave many convincing proofs that he was alive. He
appeared to them over a period of forty days and spoke
about the kingdom of God …

*I*t is not for you to know the times or dates the Father
has set by his own authority. But you will receive
power when the Holy Spirit comes on you; and you
will be my witnesses in Jerusalem, and in all Judea and
Samaria, and to the ends of the earth.

ACTS 1:7-8

*G*od so loved the world that he gave his one and only Son, that whoever believes in him shall not perish but have eternal life. For God did not send his Son into the world to condemn the world, but to save the world through him. Whoever believes in him is not condemned, but whoever does not believe stands condemned already because he has not believed in the name of God's one and only Son. This is the verdict: Light has come into the world, but men loved darkness instead of light because their deeds were evil. Everyone who does evil hates the light, and will not come into the light for fear that his deeds will be exposed. But whoever lives by the truth comes into the light, so that it may be seen plainly that what he has done has been done through God.

JOHN 3:16-21

*I*f I glorify myself, my glory means nothing. My Father ... is the one who glorifies me.

JOHN 8:54

I am the light of the world.

JOHN 9:5

A man named Lazarus was sick … [his] sisters sent word to Jesus, 'Lord, the one you love is sick' …

*T*his sickness will not end in death. No, it is for God's glory so that God's Son may be glorified through it.

JOHN 11:4

I am the resurrection and the life. He who believes in me will live, even though he dies; and whoever lives and believes in me will never die.

JOHN 11:25-6

I, when I am lifted up from the earth, will draw all men to myself.

JOHN 12:32

*W*hen the Counsellor comes, whom I will send to you from the Father, the Spirit of truth who goes out from the Father, he will testify about me. And you also must testify, for you have been with me from the beginning ...

JOHN 15:26-7

When he, the Spirit of truth, comes, he will guide you into all truth. He will not speak on his own; he will speak only what he hears, and he will tell you what is yet to come. He will bring glory to me by taking from what is mine and making it known to you. All that belongs to the Father is mine. That is why I said the Spirit will take from what is mine and make it known to you.

JOHN 16:13-15

Father, the time has come. Glorify your Son, that your Son may glorify you. For you granted him authority over all people that he might give eternal life to all those you have given him. Now this is eternal life: that they may know you, the only true God, and Jesus Christ, whom you have sent. I have brought you glory on earth by completing the work you gave me to do. And now, Father, glorify me in your presence with the glory I had with you before the world began.

JOHN 17:1-5

*M*y prayer is not for them alone. I pray also for
those who will believe in me through their message,
that all of them may be one, Father, just as you are in
me and I am in you. May they also be in us so that the
world may believe that you have sent me. I have given
them the glory that you gave me, that they may be one
as we are one: I in them and you in me. May they be
brought to complete unity to let the world know that
you sent me and have loved them even as you have
loved me.

JOHN 17:20-3

*F*ather, I want those you have given me to be with
me where I am, and to see my glory, the glory you have
given me because you loved me before the creation of
the world.

JOHN 17:24

Our Father in heaven,
hallowed be your name,
your kingdom come,
your will be done on earth as it is in heaven.
Give us today our daily bread.
Forgive us our debts,
as we also have forgiven our debtors.
And lead us not into temptation
but deliver us from the evil one.

Matthew 6:9-13

INDEX OF BIBLICAL
REFERENCES

SELECT INDEX OF MAJOR PASSAGES

Other 'In My Own Words' titles:

Cardinal Basil Hume
Compiled and edited by
Teresa de Bertodano

Basil Hume, Cardinal Archbishop of Westminster,
was an outstanding and much loved religious leader. His
death at the age of 76 saddened not only the Catholic
Church but the whole Christian community. Although first
and foremost a Roman Catholic, and a Benedictine monk,
who never compromised the reality of his own faith, his
obvious authority and holiness were felt and acknowledged
generally. He practised his faith: there was no gap between
his teaching and his life. Yet his unassuming style and the
ordinariness of his spirituality made his vision of Christ
accessible to all.

Now this little book of his teaching on all aspects of the
Christian life is a tribute to this remarkable man who always
focused on his God, never on himself, and who has left a
legacy of serenity and joy as a model for life as a Christian.

Hodder & Stoughton
ISBN 0 340 75610 1

Mother Teresa
Compiled and edited by
José Luis González-Balado

Mother Teresa's work for, and among, the poor has become
the yardstick by which millions measure compassion and
generosity across the religious divides. While Mother Teresa
herself has always stressed actions rather than words, it is
the latter that have provided solace and hope for those who
have not had the opportunity to meet her.

The quotations, stories and prayers that are collected in this
book are hers – words that she has shared with the poor, the
dying, the hurting and the sceptical, and that have moved
men and women from every race and religious background
to a new affirmation of faith.

Hodder & Stoughton
ISBN 0 340 69067 4

Pope John Paul II
Compiled and edited by
Anthony F. Chiffolo

What better spiritual guide to follow than the most travelled
pope of all time – Pope John Paul II. Quoting extensively
from a variety of sources, this book provides inspiration from
the man whose advice and insights have touched
the hearts of millions.

The collections of quotations and prayers in this book
are all his own words, compiled from material from every
area of his work and every international context. Pope John
Paul II's undying faith and concern for the human spirit
is reflected in these pages, transcending religious and
political divides.

Addressing everything from the pain of suffering to the joys
of living, these reflections emphasise the meaning and
direction of a life lived in the presence of God. This is a
wonderful series of meditations for anyone searching for
spiritual meaning in this life.

Hodder & Stoughton
ISBN 0 340 72240 1